International Financial
Reporting Standards

International Financial Reporting Standards

Belverd E. Needles, Jr.
DePaul University

Marian Powers
Northwestern University

SOUTH-WESTERN
CENGAGE Learning

Australia • Brazil • Japan • Korea • Mexico • Singapore • Spain • United Kingdom • United States

International Financial Reporting Standards, First Edition
Belverd E. Needles, Jr., Marian Powers

Vice President of Editorial, Business: Jack W. Calhoun

Editor-in-Chief: Rob Dewey

Acquisitions Editor: Matt Filimonov

Developmental Editor: Lauren Athmer

Marketing Manager: Steve Joos

Marketing Coordinator: Heather McAuliffe

Content Project Manager: Diane Bowdler

Frontlist Buyer, Manufacturing: Doug Wilke

Production Service: Integra Software Services Pvt. Ltd

Copyeditor: Maggie Sears

Compositor: Integra Software Services Pvt. Ltd

Senior Art Director: Stacy Shirley

Cover Designer: Kathy Heming

Cover Image: iStock Images

For product information and technology assistance, contact us at **Cengage Learning Customer & Sales Support, 1-800-354-9706**

For permission to use material from this text or product, submit all requests online at **cengage.com/permissions** Further permissions questions can be emailed to **permissionrequest@cengage.com**

ISBN-13: 978-0-538-74486-7
ISBN-10: 0-538-74486-3

South-Western Cengage Learning
5191 Natorp Boulevard
Mason, OH 45040
USA

Cengage Learning products are represented in Canada by Nelson Education, Ltd.

For your course and learning solutions, visit **www.cengage.com**

Purchase any of our products at your local college store or at our preferred online store **www.ichapters.com**

Printed in the United States of America
1 2 3 4 5 6 7 13 12 11 10 09

TABLE OF CONTENTS

INTERNATIONAL FINANCIAL REPORTING STANDARDS (IFRS)

INTRODUCTION: THE GLOBAL MOMENTUM FOR IFRS

For most of financial history, companies have issued financial statements based on the accounting standards of the country in which they are headquartered. As growth in the global economy expanded, companies operating worldwide became a powerful force behind efforts to achieve more uniformity in financial reporting. **International Financial Reporting Standards (IFRS)** are accounting standards set by the **International Accounting Standards Board (IASB)**, headquartered in London. Worldwide IFRS are now the most common basis of financial reporting. Over 15,000 non-United States (U.S.) listed companies currently use IFRS, and another 12,000 will likely adopt IFRS by 2012. Many foreign-based subsidiaries of U.S. multinationals operate in IFRS countries and thus prepare IFRS financial statements. With more of the world using IFRS, expectations are that the United States will follow.[1]

Through a process called convergence, the IASB is working with the U.S. **Financial Accounting Standards Board (FASB)** and other national bodies to achieve identical or nearly identical standards worldwide. The chair of the IASB predicts that by 2011 or 2012, U.S. standards and IFRS will have *converged*, that is, become much the same and that perhaps 170 countries in total will be using either U.S. standards or IFRS.[2]

The **Securities and Exchange Commission (SEC)** in the United States has pushed this campaign forward in 2007-2008 in two major ways:

- First, the SEC voted in November 2007 to allow foreign registrants in the United States to file financial statements prepared in accordance with IFRS as issued by the IASB. This change means the SEC no longer requires foreign registrants using IFRS as issued by the IASB to reconcile the differences between their financial statements and their statements using U.S. GAAP. Approximately 10 percent of all publicly listed companies in the United States are potentially impacted.[3]

- Second, the SEC approved in August 2008 and released in December 2008 a "roadmap," or timetable, that may lead to mandated use of IFRS by U.S. companies. This timetable permits selected large U.S. companies to voluntarily begin using IFRS in 2009 through 2011 and, if certain milestones are met, for others to follow in stages in 2014, 2015, and 2016 depending on a company's size.[4]

Even if one concludes that the IASB chair's convergence prediction and the SEC roadmap are overly optimistic, IFRS are now permitted in the United States for privately-held companies. In May 2008, the American Institute of CPAs (AICPA)'s governing council amended its Code of Professional Conduct to recognize the IASB as issuing high quality standards on par with

---

[1] Common acronyms used in this publication are listed in Appendix A.

[2] David Tweedie, "Simplifying Global Accounting," *Journal of Accountancy* (July, 2007).

[3] Securities and Exchange Commission, *Concept Release on Acceptance from Foreign Private Issuers of Financial Statements Prepared with International Accounting standards without Reconciliation to U.S. GAAP (Corrected)*, (August 7, 2007).

[4] Securities and Exchange Commission, *Roadmap for the Potential Use of Financial Statements Prepared in Accordance with International Financial Reporting Standards by US Issuers*, (August, 2008).

the FASB.[5] The result is that privately held companies may now choose IFRS as the basis for preparing financial statements.

Over the next few years, IFRS will likely increase in importance in both the United States and globally. Therefore, all business and accounting professionals must be knowledgeable about IFRS and their potential impact.[6]

This introduction to IFRS addresses the following topics:

    I.   The history and background of IFRS, including perceived benefits and shortcomings

    II.   The structure of IFRS and general relationship to U.S. GAAP

    III.   Key technical differences between U.S. GAAP and IFRS

    IV.   The current status of IFRS

This publication is intended to be used with any textbook and in any beginning accounting course or in any other course in which the instructor wants students to have more than a superficial knowledge of IFRS. We recommend choosing one of the following two strategies:

Strategy 1: Use as an instructional unit of one to two weeks toward the end of the course.

Strategy 2: Assign and cover Parts I and II in one class of 1 to 1 1/2 hours toward the beginning of the course and integrate the topics in Part III as they are covered in the course. Cover Part IV as a wrap-up.

In light of the complexity of this subject and the constant change in, and the development of, IFRS taking place, we view this publication as a *living* document subject to frequent revision. As a result, we welcome user feedback about its content and usefulness. Please direct your suggestions to the authors.

---

[5] American Institute of CPAs, *AICPA Council Votes to Recognize the International Accounting Standards Board as a Designated Standard Setter*, (News Release, May 18, 2008).

[6] Refer to Appendix B for a timeline of past and projected developments of IFRS since the formation of the IASB.

I. BACKGROUND OF IFRS

The goal of converging U.S. accounting standards and international standards is not of recent origin. This section explores the history of IFRS, the movement toward convergence of U.S. GAAP and IFRS, and the arguments for and against adoption of IFRS in the United States.

THE ORIGIN OF INTERNATIONAL ACCOUNTING STANDARDS (IAS)

International Accounting Standards (IAS) stem from the establishment of the **International Accounting Standard Committee (IASC)** in 1973 by the professional accountancy bodies of Australia, Canada, France, Germany, Japan, Mexico, the Netherlands, the United Kingdom and Ireland, and the United States. These bodies were members of the **International Federation of Accountants (IFAC)**, which by 1997 had 119 members in 88 countries. The individuals on the IASC were part-time and paid by the member bodies. The IASC's objectives were:

- To formulate and publish in the public interest standards to be observed in the presentation of financial statements and to promote worldwide acceptance and observance;
- To work generally for the improvement and harmonization of regulation, accounting standards and procedures relating to the presentation of financial statements.[1]

The IASC issued about twenty-five standards and worked for their acceptance. These standards were criticized as permitting too many alternative treatments intended to satisfy the great variation in accounting practices among all the members. In fact, the IASC made clear that it "endeavors not to make the International Accounting Standards so complex that they cannot be applied effectively on a worldwide basis." And that the standards are not created to "override the local regulations … governing the preparation of financial statements in a particular country."[2] In response to criticism, the IASC began work on revising the current standards into a set of "core" standards that would allow fewer alternatives.

The FASB in the United States first formally expressed interest in international standards when it issued a plan for a global focus on standard setting in 1991. Prior to this time, consideration of accounting standards in other countries was not a focus of the FASB. The FASB began to collaborate with the IASC and became a founding member of the G4+1. The G4+1 was a working group consisting of standard setters in the United Kingdom, Canada, the United States, and Australia, plus the IASC. Working outside the standard setting process, the G4+1 issued a number of policy papers related to global accounting standards. By 1998, a set of core standards had been generally agreed upon. Nevertheless, these core standards were still widely considered too broad with little specificity to various cultures. The feeling, especially among the G4+1, was that the IASC needed to have a full-time independent board. Consequently, among the most important policy papers by the G4+1 is one that urged the restructuring of the IASC to make it more independent of the member bodies.[3]

---

[1] International Accounting Standards Committee (IASC), *International Accounting Standards Explained* (West Sussex, England: Wiley, 2000), 5.

[2] International Accounting Standards Committee (IASC), IASC *Constitution (1992)*.

[3] Donna L. Street, "The Impact in the United States of Global Adoption of IFRS," *Australian Accounting Review* No. 46 Vol. 19 (Issue 3 2008), 200.

The initiative of the G4+1 led eventually to formation of the IASB in 2001. The IASB chair emphasized the historical importance of cooperation in the formation of the IASB in the following statement:

> "… the SEC and the FASB were deeply involved in the establishment of the restructured IASB, and the structure, governance, and independence of the IASB are largely modeled on the FASB's."[4]

The IASB is an independent standard-setting board and does not represent any particular country, and is not part of any other international bodies such as IFAC.[5] The structure and oversight of the IASB is shown in Figure 1. Members of the IASB work full-time and must give up any affiliations to other organizations. Its organization is illustrated in Figure 1. The goal of the IASB is "to provide the world's integrating capital markets with a common language for financial reporting." Its output is intended to be high quality, enforceable, global standards.[6]

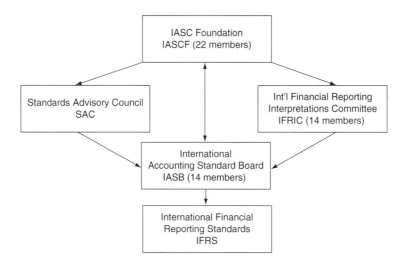

Figure 1: IASB Structure

Appointing and overseeing the IASB is the **IASC Foundation (IASCF)**, a not-for-profit, private sector body consisting of a geographically and professionally diverse group of twenty-two trustees who are accountable to the public interest. To support the IASB's budget of approximately $24 million in 2008, the IASCF also raises funds from thousands of bodies who benefit from the standards and by mandatory levies for listed and non-listed companies in many countries. It also receives official support from relevant regulatory authorities. Further, the IASCF appoints support committees to the IASB, such as the **International Financial Reporting Interpretation Committee (IFRIC)** and the **Standards Advisory Council (SAC)**. The IFRIC issues interpretations of IFRS, also developed by due process, when divergent practices have emerged regarding the accounting for particular transactions or circumstance or when there

---

[4] David Tweedie, "Simplifying Global Accounting," *Journal of Accountancy* (July, 2007).

[5] This section is development from information on the International Accounting Standards Committee (IASB) website, http://www.IASB.org.

[6] International Accounting Standards Board, *Preface to International Financial Reporting Standards* (http://www.eIFRS.org).

is doubt about the appropriate accounting treatment. The IFRIC replaces the **Standards Interpretation Committee (SIC)** under the IASC. The SAC, which consists of a wide-range of representatives from user groups, financial analysts, academics, auditors, regulators, and professional accounting bodies, advises the IFRS on a broad range of issues, including the IASB's agenda and work program. The SAC also reports to the IASC Foundation on its work and its evaluation of the IASC.

IFRS are developed through the due process illustrated in Figure 2. Steps followed in achieving due process are as follows:

1. The IASB and staff set an agenda of possible issues to be addressed by IFRS.
2. Once an issue is deemed worthy of study, the project is planned including deciding if it will be a joint project with other bodies such as the FASB.
3. After research and discussion by the IASB and staff, a discussion paper (DP) is prepared for public discussion.
4. After considering all comments and additional proposals to its DP, the board may issue an exposure draft (ED) for further public consideration, as in (1).
5. These further comments are considered. IASB may at this point publish a final IFRS to be considered for adoption in the various jurisdictions.
6. After two years, a post-implementation review of the IFRS is conducted by the board.

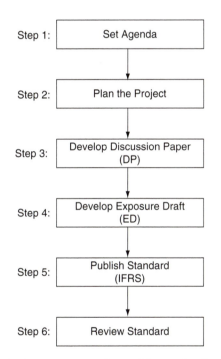

Figure 2: Due Process Steps if Developing IFRS

This thorough, open, and transparent process led to widespread acceptance of IFRS throughout the world. The European Union mandated use of IFRS for companies engaged in international markets beginning with 2005 financial statements. Germany's adherence was deferred until 2007. Also, by 2007, Australia, Brazil, Canada, Chile, India, Japan, Korea, and New Zealand, among others, had adopted timelines to adopt or converge with IFRS. Today, more than 100 countries require or permit the use of IFRS.

The FASB and the IASB mutually issued a **Memorandum of Understanding (MOU)** in 2002 that laid out a joint commitment of cooperation:

- To make their existing financial reporting standards fully compatible as soon as is practical and
- To coordinate future work programs to ensure that once achieved, compatibility is maintained.[7]

The two bodies reaffirmed their commitment to convergence in 2005. Also, in that year the SEC joined with the **European Commission (EC)** with a similar goal by producing a *Roadmap to Convergence* agreement. The roadmap specified the steps that should occur before the elimination of the requirement for foreign registrants reporting to reconcile their statements' net income and stockholders' equity to U.S. GAAP could be eliminated. A New York City report suggested the city could lose its world financial center within ten years without a major shift in policy and regulation, including recognition by the SEC of IFRS without the reconciliation for foreign SEC registrants and the promoting of global converge of accounting standards.[8] This action would eliminate unnecessary costs and remove a barrier for foreign issuers. Companies, investors, rating agencies, accounting firms, and others echoed these sentiments leading to the SEC decision in November 2007 to drop the reconciliation requirement for foreign registrants that used IFRS.[9]

Since March 2007, the SEC has held three roundtables to examine IFRS. In August 2008, the SEC voted to publish for public comment a proposed further roadmap that could lead to the use of IFRS by U.S. issuers beginning in 2014. The decision as to whether to mandate IFRS for U.S. public companies is expected in 2011. The SEC believes that a common accounting language around the world could give investors greater comparability and greater confidence in the transparency of financial reporting worldwide.[10] A common accounting language could potentially lower the cost of capital and avoid the cost of preparing statements on multiple standards. The roadmap sets out a series of milestones that, if achieved, could lead to the positive decision, as follows:

- Improvements in accounting standards
- Accountability and funding of the IFSC Foundation
- Improvement in the ability to use interactive data for IFRS reporting
- Education and Training in the United States relating to IFRS
- The anticipated timing of future rulemaking by the commission
- Potential implementation of the mandatory use of IFRS, including considerations relating to whether any mandatory use of IFRS should be staged or sequenced among groups of companies based on their market capitalization

---

[7] *Memorandum of Understanding between the FASB and the IASB, September 2002.*

[8] Schumer, C. and M. Bloomberg, *Sustaining New York's and The US' Global Financial Services Leadership*, www.senate.gov/schumer, 2007.

[9] Donna L. Street, "The Impact in the United States of Global Adoption of IFRS," *Australian Accounting Review* No. 46 Vol. 19 (Issue 3 2008), 200–201.

[10] "SEC Proposes Roadmap toward Global Accounting Standards to Help Investors Compare Financial Information More Easily," SEC Press Release, 2008, 184.

The large CPA firms, the AICPA, and many others strongly support the adoption of IFRS for use by U.S. public companies. However, barriers to acceptance voiced by industry groups and individual experts exist. Let's examine some arguments for and against adopting IFRS for U.S. registrants.[11]

Reasons Favoring the Use of IFRS by U.S. Public Companies

1. *IFRS would enhance comparability among companies globally.* When financial statements are prepared using the same set of standards, investors and other users will be able to more readily assess performance and to make comparisons among companies, especially in such industries as banking, insurance, motor vehicles, pharmaceuticals, and telecommunications.

2. *IFRS presents opportunities to global U.S. companies.* Among the benefits to be gained are lower costs through standardization of financial reporting, centralization of processes, improved controls, and better cash management.

3. *All SEC registrants should be provided the same options, not just foreign filers.* For example, the U.S. technology industry could be harmed because IFRS may provide more flexibility in the timing of revenue recognition than under U.S. GAAP.

4. *Use of IFRS by U.S. companies would enhance transparency and global comparability of financial reports.* By having financial statements that are more in conformity with the rest of the world, U.S. companies would be more competitive in global capital markets, thus, lowering their cost of capital.

Reasons For Not Using IFRS by U.S. Public Companies

1. *In spite of efforts at convergence, significant differences between IFRS and U.S. GAAP remain.* A significant body of research shows that, if anything, the reporting differences between U.S. companies using U.S. GAAP and foreign companies using IFRS has increased.[12] For instance, one study showed that net income under IFRS was higher than under U.S. GAAP and that the difference between 2004 IFRS and U.S. GAAP net income significantly exceed the difference between European GAAP and U.S. GAAP net income. Further, a survey by a major bank yielded similar results supporting their conclusion that the two sets of standards cause major swings in net income. On average, IFRS net income was 23 percent higher than U.S. GAAP net income.

2. *IASB needs to be strengthened as an independent, global standard setter.* The IASB needs to establish ways to ensure stability of funding and staffing as well as enforcement in countries where IFRS are adopted only as they suit local reporting traditions.

3. *Significant changes to the U.S. reporting infrastructure are needed to support the move to IFRS.* Among these are to 1) train and educate issuers, regulators, auditors, and

---

[11] These sections are based on Donna L. Street, "The Impact in the United States of Global Adoption of IFRS," *Australian Accounting Review*, No. 46 Vol. 18 Issue 3 (2008), 199–208.

[12] Donna L. Street, "The Impact in the United States of Global Adoption of IFRS," *Australian Accounting Review* No. 46 Vol. 19 (Issue 3 2008), 202–203.

investors about IFRS, 2) transition auditing standards, 3) adjust regulatory and contractual arrangements, and 4) assess impact on non-public companies, not-for-profit organizations, and specialized industry reporting. It will take a number of years to accomplish these changes.

4. *U.S. accountants are not adequately versed in IFRS.* Unprecedented changes in curriculum at colleges and universities and a substantial increase in continuing professional education for those already in practice are required. Also, practice indicates a stiff learning curve for many first-time users of IFRS

5. *All U.S. companies should use the same standards and not given an option to use IFRS.* Lobbying to keep certain widespread U.S. practices is likely. For example, IFRS does not and is not expected to allow use of LIFO, a method of accounting for inventories used by most U.S. companies. A change to other inventory methods would likely cause significant tax and cash flow consequences.

6. *Improvements in IFRS are needed.* U.S. GAAP has a longer history and is more comprehensive than IFRS. Joint IASB/FASB projects will take years to complete. Also, it is unclear what will happen with reporting and disclosure topics not covered by IFRS.

7. *Continued existence of European IFRS destroys all hopes for convergence and a global set of accounting standards.* Research has shown that European countries that adopt IFRS tend to place their own interpretations on them. Since IFRS are "principles-based" and do not have great detail there is room for each country to apply them in their own way. At times European regulators simply ignore aspects of IFRS. For example, French regulators do not follow IFRS in accounting for financial instruments. If companies using IFRS from different European countries produce financial statements that lack comparability, why would adoption by the United States achieve the goal of more comparability? Also, some fear in Europe exists that efforts of the IASB to work with the FASB will have too much influence on U.S. practices.

8. *Elimination of U.S. GAAP utilized by U.S. companies contradicts the general sentiment in the United States that by maintaining control of setting accounting standards, the influence of the FASB, SEC and other U.S. organizations would be limited or nonexistent.* Many are unwilling to give ultimate power in financial reporting to a body in a foreign country. What will happen if the IASB fails to act on an issue vital to U.S. interests? How would such conflicts be resolved?

9. *IFRS are not a comprehensive set of standards suitable for the U.S. market.* As mentioned above, IFRS does not cover many areas existing in U.S. GAAP. For example, the SEC will need a plan for industries where U.S. GAAP provides industry-specific standards. Also, IFRS allows flexibility in the application of standards. Without guidance, comparability will be greatly impeded.

10. *Enhanced lobbying will limit the IASB's ability to maintain IFRS' status as principles-based and thus prevent the desired move from the current U.S. approach of providing extensive guidance.* The IASB has a short history. As it becomes older and more powerful, strong forces will inevitably arise that will force it to address more specific issues of implementation. If it does not, then a wide variety of practices will develop around the world and the goal of comparability motivating the switch to IFRS will be lost.

Thus, will the IFRS live up to their promise? The answer is "maybe." Certainly, the movement to switch to IFRS has support and momentum. However, challenges remain and the economic crisis may delay completion of the roadmap. The convergence project of the FASB and IASB must continue with great haste while the IASB works to improve IFRS for adoption in the United States. Further, the SEC may delay its plans for implementation of IFRS while it considers the costs and benefits of adoption, as well as the steps needed to improve comparability under IFRS.[13]

REVIEW QUESTIONS

1. What international organization began the movement toward international accounting standards and when and how did the United States become involved?
2. What is the IASB; when was the IASB formed; and why is its structure important?
3. Briefly, what is the process followed by the IASB for issuing an IFRS?
4. What is the Memorandum of Understanding (MOU) and why is it important?
5. What is the SEC roadmap and why is it important?
6. What conditions must the IASB meet in order for adoption of IFRS by the United States in 2011? List one or two conditions that will be the most difficult to accomplish.
7. In your opinion, what are the two most important arguments in favor of allowing IFRS for U.S. public companies?
8. In your opinion, what are the two most important arguments against allowing IFRS for public U.S. companies?
9. *Class or group discussion*: Should the SEC require U.S. public companies to use IFRS?

---

[13] "New SEC Chair May delay IFRS Roadmap," *WebCPA*, January 16, 2009.

II. THE STRUCTURE OF IFRS

This section summarizes the structure and approach of IFRS and then identifies the major types of differences between IFRS and U.S. GAAP.

OVERVIEW OF IFRS

The IASB achieves its objectives primarily by developing and publishing IFRS and promoting the use of those standards in general purpose financial statements and other financial reporting. IFRS typically require like transactions and events to be accounted for and reported similarly and unlike transactions and events to be accounted for and reported differently, both within an entity over time and among entities. Although some choices currently exist, the IASB intends not to permit choices in accounting treatment.

IFRS are designed to apply to all profit-oriented entities. Profit-oriented entities include those engaged in commercial, industrial, financial and similar activities, whether organized in corporate or in other forms. A complete set of financial statements includes the following:

- Balance sheet
- Income statement
- Statement showing either all changes in equity or changes in equity other than those arising from capital transactions with owners and distributions to owners
- Cash flow statement
- Accounting policies and explanatory notes

These financial statements are directed toward the common information needs of a wide range of users such as shareholders, creditors, employees, and the public at large.

Financial statements must not be described as complying with IFRS unless they comply with *all* the requirements of IFRS. Mandatory IFRS comprise the following and are listed in Appendix C:

- IFRS issued by the IASB currently consist of eight standards issued since the formation of the IASB in 2001.
- IAS issued by the IASC from its beginning in 1971 that have not been superseded by the IFRS. Currently of the original forty-one IAS, twenty-nine are still in effect.
- Interpretations originated by the IFRIC or its predecessor, the SIC. Currently, eleven IFRIC and eleven SIC are still in effect.

Downloadable electronic educational versions of IFRS are available to both faculty and students of the **International Association for Accounting Education and Research (IAAER)** for a nominal membership fee. IAAER is the global association of academic accountants. Its website is http://www.iaaer.org.

FRAMEWORK FOR THE PREPARATION AND PRESENTATION OF FINANCIAL STATEMENTS[1]

To aid in the development of future IAS and in the review of existing IAS, the IASC issued the *Framework for the Preparation and Presentation of Financial Statements* for external users. The IASB continues to rely on the framework in setting IFRS. The purpose of the framework is to set forth the basic concepts that underlie financial statements. Thus it provides guidance to the IASB when setting standards as well as for preparers in interpreting and applying IFRS. Importantly, the framework is not an IAS or IFRS, and hence, does not define standards for any particular measurement or disclosure issue. Nothing in the framework overrides any specific standard. The framework is currently under revision by the IASB.

The framework defines the following:

- Objective of financial statements
- Qualitative characteristics
- Definition, recognition, and measurement of the elements from which financial statements are constructed
- Concepts of capital and capital maintenance

Financial statements are frequently described as showing a true and fair view of, or as presenting fairly, the financial position, performance, and changes in financial position of an entity. The framework does not deal directly with such concepts, but the application of the concepts in this framework to the accounting standards is intended to result in financial statements that convey what is generally understood as a true and fair view of, or as presenting fairly, such information.

OBJECTIVE OF FINANCIAL STATEMENTS

The objective of financial statements is to provide information about the financial position, performance, and changes in financial position of an entity that is useful to a wide range of users in making economic decisions. The objective is not to provide all information necessary to make economic decisions. Financial statements, for example, are based on past information and do not normally provide projections of future information or non-financial information. Financial statements also show the results of the stewardship of management, or the accountability of management for the resources entrusted to it.

Two assumptions underlying financial statements are **accrual accounting** and **going concern**. Accrual accounting assumes that information is most useful when the effects of transactions and other events are recognized when they occur (and not as cash or its equivalent is received or paid) and that they are recorded in the accounting records and reported in the financial statements of the periods to which they relate. Financial statements prepared on the accrual basis inform users not only of past transactions involving the payment and receipt of cash, but also of obligations to pay cash in the future and of resources that represent cash to be received in the future. The going concern assumption presumes that the company will continue in operation for the foreseeable future, thus allowing judgments to be made about the future on which the financial statements are based.

---

[1] This section is based on IASB, *Framework for the Preparation and Presentation of Financial Statements*, http://www.iasb.org, October 2008.

Qualitative characteristics are the attributes that make the information provided in financial statements useful to users. The four principal qualitative characteristics are as follows:

- **Understandability**: Information has the quality of understandability if users readily understand it. Users are assumed to have a reasonable knowledge of business, economic activities, and accounting as well as a willingness to study the information with reasonable diligence. However, relevant information about complex matters should not be excluded merely on the grounds that it may be too difficult for certain users to understand.

- **Relevance**: Information has the quality of relevance when it influences users' economic decisions, aiding their evaluation of past, present or future events, or confirming or correcting their past evaluations. In some cases, the *nature* of information alone is sufficient to determine its relevance, such as the reporting of a new segment. In other cases, *materiality* is important. Information is **material** if its omission or misstatement could influence the user's economic decisions taken on the basis of the financial statements. Materiality is related to the size of an item or misstatement and provides a threshold or cut-off point rather than being a primary qualitative characteristic.

- **Reliability**: Information has the quality of reliability when it is free from material error and bias and can be depended upon by users to represent faithfully that which it either purports to represent or could reasonably be expected to represent. Reliability is a complex concept that implies the following:

  - *Faithful representation*: Most financial information is subject to some risk of being less than a faithful representation of that which it purports to portray. This risk is not due to bias, but rather to inherent difficulties either in identifying the transactions and other events to be measured or in devising and applying measurement and presentation techniques that can convey messages that correspond with those transactions and events. Where possible, the risk of error surrounding recognition and measurement of items should be disclosed.

  - *Substance over form*: If information is to represent the transactions and other events that it purports to represent faithfully, it is necessary that these transactions and other events are accounted for and presented in accordance with their substance and economic reality and not merely their legal form.

  - *Neutrality*: To be neutral, the information contained in financial statements must be free from bias. There must be no deliberate slanting or misstatement of information.

  - *Prudence*: To be prudent, a degree of caution in the exercise of the judgments is needed in making the estimates required under conditions of uncertainty, such that assets or income are not overstated and liabilities or expenses are not understated. However, the exercise of prudence does not allow, for example, the creation of hidden reserves or excessive provisions, the deliberate understatement of assets or income, or the deliberate overstatement of liabilities or expenses, because the financial statements would not be neutral and, therefore, would not have the quality of reliability.

- **Comparability**: Information has the quality of comparability if users may compare the financial statements of an entity through time in order to identify trends and also compare the financial statements of different entities in order to evaluate their relative financial position, performance, and changes in financial position. This quality implies that like transactions and other events are carried out consistently throughout an entity and over time for that entity and for different entities. Lack of consistency should be disclosed to the users.

In achieving a balance among the qualities, the overriding consideration is how best to satisfy the economic decision-making needs of users. Tradeoffs may be acceptable. The aim is to achieve an appropriate balance among the characteristics in order to meet the objective of financial statements. The relative importance of the characteristics in different cases is a matter of professional judgment. For example, *timeliness* relates to the trade-off between waiting until information is highly reliable at the expense of relevance. To provide information on a timely basis it may often be necessary to report before all aspects of a transaction or other event are known, thus impairing reliability. Conversely, if reporting is delayed until all aspects are known, the information may be highly reliable but of little use to users who have had to make decisions in the interim. Also, *cost-benefit* refers to the need for benefits derived from information to exceed the cost of providing it. Although it is difficult to apply a cost-benefit test in any particular case, standard-setters, preparers, and users of financial statements should be aware of this constraint.

APPLICATION OF CONCEPTUAL FRAMEWORK TO FAIR VALUE

Fair value underlies the measurement of all items under IFRS. Fair value is the amount for which an asset could be exchanged, or a liability settled, between knowledgeable parties in an arm's length transaction. According to one member of the IASB, fair values

- Are *relevant* because they reflect conditions relating to economic resources and obligations, under which financial statement users will make decisions.
- Have *predictive value* because they help predict future cash flows of interest to investors in valuing equity.
- Can be *faithful representations* of assets and liabilities because they reflect risk and probability-weighted assessments of expected future cash flows.
- Are *neutral* because they are unbiased.
- Are *timely* because they reflect changes in economic conditions.
- Are *comparable* because fair value depends only on the characteristics of the asset or liability being measured, not on the characteristics of the entity holding the asset or liability or when it was acquired.
- Enhance *consistency*, a dimension of comparability, because they reflect the same type of information every period.[2]

PROPOSED PRESENTATION OF FINANCIAL STATEMENTS[3]

A goal of the MOU between the IASB and the FASB is to create a common standard for the form, content, classification, aggregation, and display of items in financial statements. The boards developed three objectives for financial statement presentation:

- To portray a cohesive picture of an entity's activities. "Cohesion" means that to the extent possible, the categories and sections in the financial statements should be in

---

[2] Mary M. Barth, "Global Financial Reporting: Implication for U.S. Academics," *The Accounting Review*, Vol. 83, No. 5 (September 2008), 1165.

[3] This section is based on Financial Accounting Standards Board (FASB), "Preliminary Views on Financial Statement Presentation," *Financial Accounting Series Discussion Paper* (October 16, 2008). Comments on the proposed presentations were due by April 14, 2009.

the same order so that the relationships between items across financial statements are clear.

- To disaggregate information so that it is useful in predicting an entity's future cash flows.
- To help users assess an entity's liquidity and financial flexibility. Users should be able to assess an entity's ability to meet its financial commitments, invest in business opportunities, and respond to unexpected needs.[4]

It addresses only the organization and presentation of information and the need for totals and subtotals in the financial statements. It does not address any issues of recognition or measurement of the individual items included in the statements. This work is being completed in three phases:

- **Phase A:** Issuance by the IASB of a revision of its IAS No. 1, *Presentation of Financial Statements*. Phase A was completed in 2007. This revision calls for four financial statements, each with at least two years of comparative data, as follows:
  - Statement of comprehensive income
  - Statement of financial position
  - Statement of cash flows
  - Statement of changes in equity

- **Phase B:** Completed in 2008, Phase B presents tentative and preliminary views on how financial information should be presented in the financial statements.

- **Phase C:** The goal of Phase C is to arrive at converged standards on financial statements presentation by 2011. The boards will also work on the presentation of interim financial information.

Phase B addresses the goal of showing a cohesive financial picture of an entity through financial statement presentation. All similar line items across the statements should be labeled in the same way and in the same order. The joint task force proposed a structure, as shown in Exhibit 1, for achieving this objective of cohesion across the statements. Note that all proposed statements follow roughly the current organization of the statement of cash flows. All statements will be divided into five categories as follows:

- Business: Includes line items related to operating and investing activities.
- Financing: Includes line items related to financing activities.
- Income taxes
- Discontinued operations
- Equity

PROPOSED STATEMENT OF COMPREHENSIVE INCOME

The proposed parallel classification scheme of the financial statements is shown in Table 1. Management chooses what goes into each category and explains its choices in the accounting policy note to the financial statements. Note that joint task force provided the illustrations for discussion and that the final statement formats may differ.

Exhibit 1 illustrates the five-part classification scheme in the proposed statement of comprehensive income. Note first that the statement's title now includes the words *comprehensive*

---

[4] Memorandum of Understanding between the FASB and the IASB, February 2007.

Table 1: Parallel Classification Scheme of the Financial Statements

Statement of Comprehensive Income	Statement of Financial Position	Statement of Cash Flows
Business • Operating income and expense • Investing income and expense	**Business** • Operating assets and liabilities • Investing assets and liabilities	**Business** • Operating cash flows • Investing cash flows
Financing • Financing asset income • Financing liability expense	**Financing** • Financing assets • Financing liabilities	**Financing** • Financing asset cash flows • Financing liability cash flows
Income Taxes (relating to business and financing)	**Income Taxes (deferred and payable)**	**Income Taxes (cash taxes paid)**
Discontinued Operations, Net of Tax	**Discontinued Operations**	**Discontinued Operations**
Other Comprehensive Income, Net of Tax	**Equity (Share capital, retained earnings, other comprehensive income)**	**Equity**

income, indicating that it will include items that previously were disclosed separately as other comprehensive income. (IFRS allows for the option of presenting comprehensive income in a separate statement.) It is important to note that IFRS specifies minimal information on this statement. Only six lines are required:

- Revenue
- Finance costs
- Share of profit and loss from equity method
- Tax expense
- Discontinued operations
- Profit or loss

However, except for this last section of the statement disclosing other comprehensive income, the other sections are not dramatically different for the traditional income statement. Use of the word *net profit* is used where the word *net income* is traditionally used.

The following characterize the considerable detail of *business section*:

- Cost of goods sold is deducted from sales to reach gross profit.
- Selling expenses are separated from general and administrative expenses.
- Other operating income (expense) includes various gains and losses as well as the share of any associate (controlling investments) profit.
- Total operating income is a subtotal.
- Income and gains from investing activities including the share of any associate (less than controlling investments) profit are shown after total operating income.
- The bottom line of the business section is *total business income*.

Exhibit 1: ToolCo Financial Statements (Proposed Format)
STATEMENT OF COMPREHENSIVE INCOME

	For the year ended 31 December	
	2010	**2009**
BUSINESS		
Operating		
Sales—wholesale	2,790,080	2,591,400
Sales—retail	697,520	647,850
Total revenue	*3,487,600*	*3,239,250*
Cost of goods sold		
Materials	(1,043,100)	(925,000)
Labour	(405,000)	(450,000)
Overhead—depreciation	(219,300)	(215,000)
Overhead—transport	(128,640)	(108,000)
Overhead—other	(32,160)	(27,000)
Change in inventory	(60,250)	(46,853)
Pension	(51,975)	(47,250)
Loss on obsolete and damaged inventory	(29,000)	(9,500)
Total cost of goods sold	*(1,969,425)*	*(1,828,603)*
Gross profit	*1,518,175*	*1,410,647*
Selling expenses		
Advertising	(60,000)	(50,000)
Wages, salaries, and benefits	(56,700)	(52,500)
Bad debt	(23,068)	(15,034)
Other	(13,500)	(12,500)
Total selling expenses	*(153,268)*	*(130,034)*
General and administrative expenses		
Wages, salaries, and benefits	(321,300)	(297,500)
Depreciation	(59,820)	(58,500)
Pension	(51,975)	(47,250)
Share-based remuneration	(22,023)	(17,000)
Interest on lease liability	(14,825)	(16,500)
Research and development	(8,478)	(7,850)
Other	(15,768)	(14,600)
Total general and administrative expenses	*(494,189)*	*(459,200)*
Income before other operating items	*870,718*	*821,413*
Other operating income (expense)		
Share of profit of associate A	23,760	22,000
Gain on disposal of property, plant and equipment	22,650	-
Realized gain on cash flow hedge	3,996	3,700
Loss on sale of receivables	(4,987)	(2,025)
Impairment loss on goodwill	-	(35,033)

	For the year ended 31 December	
	2010	**2009**
Total other operating income (expense)	*45,419*	*(11,358)*
Total operating income	**916,137**	**810,055**
Investing		
Dividend income	54,000	50,000
Realized gain on available-for-sale securities	18,250	7,500
Share of profit of associate B	7,500	3,250
Total investing income	**79,750**	**60,750**
TOTAL BUSINESS INCOME	**995,887**	**870,805**
FINANCING		
Interest income on cash	8,619	5,500
Total financing asset income	**8,619**	**5,500**
Interest expense	(111,352)	(110,250)
Total financing liability expense	**(111,352)**	**(110,250)**
TOTAL NET FINANCING EXPENSE	**(102,733)**	**(104,750)**
Profit from continuing operations before taxes and other comprehensive income	*893,154*	*766,055*
INCOME TAXES		
Income tax expense	(333,625)	(295,266)
Net profit from continuing operations	*559,529*	*470,789*
DISCONTINUED OPERATIONS		
Loss on discontinued operations	(32,400)	(35,000)
Tax benefit	11,340	12,250
NET LOSS FROM DISCONTINUED OPERATIONS	**(21,060)**	**(22,750)**
NET PROFIT	**538,469**	**448,039**
OTHER COMPREHENSIVE INCOME (after tax)		
Unrealized gain on available-for-sale securities (investing)	17,193	15,275
Revaluation surplus (operating)	3,653	-
Foreign currency translation adjust—consolidated subsidiary	2,094	(1,492)
Unrealized gain on cash flow hedge (operating)	1,825	1,690
Foreign currency translation adjust—associate A (operating)	(1,404)	(1,300)
TOTAL OTHER COMPREHENSIVE INCOME	**23,361**	**14,173**
TOTAL COMPREHENSIVE INCOME	**561,830**	**462,212**
Basic earnings per share	7.07	6.14
Diluted earnings per share	6.85	5.96

Source: IASB, *Preliminary Views on Financial Statement Presentation,* October 2008.

IFRS do not define operating income, allowing companies some flexibility in format. For instance, IFRS allow the order and detail of the line items in this section to be organized by function (cost of goods sold, gross profit, operating expenses, as illustrated) or by the nature of the expense (not illustrated) such as materials, labor, overhead, bad debt expense, and so forth.

The *financing section* consists of interest income on cash and interest expense.

The *income taxes section* consists of incomes tax expense.

The *discontinued operations section* consists of income, gains, or losses on discontinued operations including showing the tax effect.

Finally, the *other comprehensive section* consists of such items as:

- Unrealized gains on available-for-sale securities
- Revaluation surplus
- Foreign currency translation adjustments
- Unrealized gains on cash-flow hedges

PROPOSED STATEMENT OF FINANCIAL POSITION

Exhibit 2, which shows a proposed statement of financial position (balance sheet), demonstrates the radical change that the above-described approach makes to the traditional form of the balance sheet. No longer will assets and liabilities be on opposite sides of the balance sheet. On the contrary, the following will characterize the *business section*:

- Both short-term and long-term assets and liabilities will be presented.
- The short-term section will first list receivables, inventories, and prepaid assets (cash is not included) followed by a deduction for accounts payable and other current liabilities.
- The long-term section lists property, plant, and equipment, goodwill, intangibles, and other assets and liabilities (net).
- The long-term section includes available-for-sale securities and other long-term investments including investments in affiliates.
- The bottom line for the business section is *net business assets*.

The *financing section* will be characterized by the following:

- Cash will no longer include cash equivalents and will be considered a financing asset.
- Financing liabilities will include both short-term and long-term liabilities not included elsewhere.
- The bottom line for the financing section is *net financing assets* (or *liabilities* if the balance is negative).

The *income taxes section* will consist of:

- Short-term income taxes payable
- Long-term deferred income taxes (net)
- The bottom line for the income taxes section is *net income tax* assets (or *liabilities* if the balance is negative*).

The *discontinued operations section* will consist of:

- Assets classified as held for sale
- Liabilities classified as held for sale
- The bottom line for the discontinued operations section is *net assets held for sale.*

Exhibit 2: ToolCo Financial Statements (Proposed Format)
STATEMENT OF FINANCIAL POSITION

	As at 31 December	
	2010	**2009**
BUSINESS		
Operating		
Accounts receivable, trade	945,678	541,375
Less allowance for doubtful accounts	(23,642)	(13,534)
Accounts receivable, net	922,036	527,841
Inventory	679,474	767,102
Prepaid advertising	80,000	75,000
Foreign exchange contracts—cash flow hedge	6,552	3,150
Total short-term assets	*1,688,062*	*1,373,092*
Property, plant and equipment	5,112,700	5,088,500
Less accumulated depreciation	(2,267,620)	(2,023,500)
Property, plant and equipment, net	2,845,080	3,065,000
Investment in associate A	261,600	240,000
Goodwill	154,967	154,967
Other intangible assets	35,000	35,000
Total long-term assets	*3,296,647*	*3,494,967*
Accounts payable, trade	(612,556)	(505,000)
Advances from customers	(182,000)	(425,000)
Wages payable	(173,000)	(200,000)
Share-based remuneration liability	(39,586)	(21,165)
Current portion of lease liability	(35,175)	(33,500)
Interest payable on lease liability	(14,825)	(16,500)
Total short-term liabilities	*(1,057,142)*	*(1,201,165)*
Accrued pension liability	(293,250)	(529,500)
Lease liability (excluding current portion)	(261,325)	(296,500)
Other long-term liabilities	(33,488)	(16,100)
Total long-term liabilities	*(588,063)*	*(842,100)*
Net operating assets	**3,339,504**	**2,824,795**
Investing		
Available-for-sale financial assets (short-term)	473,600	485,000
Investment in associate B (long-term)	46,750	39,250
Total investing assets	**520,350**	**524,250**
NET BUSINESS ASSETS	**3,859,854**	**3,349,045**
FINANCING		
Financing assets		
Cash	1,174,102	861,941
Total financing assets	**1,174,102**	**861,941**

(*Continued*)

STATEMENT OF FINANCIAL POSITION

	As at 31 December	
	2010	2009
Financing liabilities		
Short-term borrowings	(562,000)	(400,000)
Interest payable	(140,401)	(112,563)
Dividends payable	(20,000)	(20,000)
Total short-term financing liabilities	*(722,401)*	*(532,563)*
Long-term borrowings	(2,050,000)	(2,050,000)
Total financing liabilities	**(2,772,401)**	**(2,582,563)**
NET FINANCING LIABILITIES	**(1,598,299)**	**(1,720,621)**
DISCONTINUED OPERATIONS		
Assets held for sale	856,832	876,650
Liabilities related to assets held for sale	(400,000)	(400,000)
NET ASSETS HELD FOR SALE	**456,832**	**476,650**
INCOME TAXES		
Short-term		
Deferred tax asset	4,426	8,907
Income taxes payable	(72,514)	(63,679)
Long-term		
Deferred tax asset	39,833	80,160
NET INCOME TAX ASSET (LIABILITY)	**(28,255)**	**25,388**
NET ASSETS	*2,690,132*	*2,130,462*
EQUITY		
Share capital	(1,427,240)	(1,343,000)
Retained earnings	(1,100,358)	(648,289)
Accumulated other comprehensive income, net	(162,534)	(139,173)
TOTAL EQUITY	**(2,690,132)**	**(2,130,462)**
Total short-term assets	**4,197,021**	**3,605,591**
Total long-term assets	**3,383,231**	**3,614,377**
Total assets	**7,580,252**	**7,219,968**
Total short-term liabilities	**(2,252,057)**	**(2,197,406)**
Total long-term liabilities	**(2,638,063)**	**(2,892,100)**
Total liabilities	**(4,890,120)**	**(5,089,506)**

Source: IASB, *Preliminary Views on Financial Statement Presentation,* October 2008.

Finally, the *equity section* will consist of:

- Common stock and additional paid-in capital
- Treasury stock, retained earnings
- Accumulated other comprehensive income
- The bottom line for the equity section is *total equity*.

PROPOSED STATEMENT OF CASH FLOWS

The statement of cash flows, as illustrated in Exhibit 3, is similar to the traditional statement of cash flows, except for the following:

- The direct method is used in preparing the operating section, which begins with cash received form sales and is divided into several operating categories with subtotals, such as cash paid for goods sold, selling activities, general and administration activities, and other operating activities.
- Income taxes and discontinued operations are set out separately as they were in the balance sheet and statement of comprehensive income.

The indirect method (starting with net income and reconciling to cash flow from operating activities) is required as an additional disclosure under FAS No. 95. The need for this disclosure is being evaluated in light of the proposed disclosure described in the next paragraph.

PROPOSED STATEMENT OF CHANGES IN EQUITY

Exhibit 4, on page 24, illustrates the statement of changes in equity for the two years. This statement is similar to the statement of stockholders' equity used under U.S. GAAP in that it shows all changes in equity during each year.

PROPOSED RECONCILIATION OF CASH FLOWS TO COMPREHENSIVE INCOME

A proposed new reconciliation of cash flows to comprehensive income, shown in Exhibit 5 (pages 25-29), is intended to provide investors, creditors, and analysts with information that is useful in predicting cash flows. This schedule shows only the reconciliation for the year ended December 31, 2010. In practice, a similar schedule is needed for each year presented. It begins with the cash flow under the direct method (Column A) and reconciles it to the comprehensive income (Column E). The other columns show reconciling items for non-remeasurements (Column B: accruals, allocations, and other charges), remeasurements including adjustments for changes in fair value (Column C), and other remeasurements (Column D). Remeasurements will be discussed in a later section. The value and format of this reconciling disclosure is sure to be debated and will likely have changes before being formally adopted by the IASB and FASB.

The FASB and IASB project team, which is now joined by the Accounting Standards Board of Japan (ASBJ), will work on Phase C, which, in addition to working toward converged standards, will address such issues as the format of interim financial statements, comparative periods, and reporting by nonpublic companies.

Exhibit 3: ToolCo Financial Statements (Proposed Format)
STATEMENT OF CASH FLOWS

	For the year ended 31 December	
	2010	**2009**
BUSINESS		
Operating		
Cash received from wholesale customers	2,108,754	1,928,798
Cash received from retail customers	703,988	643,275
Total cash collected from customers	*2,812,742*	*2,572,073*
Cash paid for goods		
Materials purchases	(935,544)	(785,000)
Labour	(418,966)	(475,313)
Overhead—transport	(128,640)	(108,000)
Pension	(170,100)	(157,500)
Overhead—other	(32,160)	(27,000)
Total cash paid for goods	*(1,685,409)*	*(1,552,813)*
Cash paid for selling activities		
Advertising	(65,000)	(75,000)
Wages, salaries, and benefits	(58,655)	(55,453)
Other	(13,500)	(12,500)
Total cash paid for selling activities	*(137,155)*	*(142,953)*
Cash paid for general and administrative activities		
Wages, salaries, and benefits	(332,379)	(314,234)
Contributions to pension plan	(170,100)	(157,500)
Capital expenditures	(54,000)	(50,000)
Lease payments	(50,000)	-
Research and development	(8,478)	(7,850)
Settlement of share-based remuneration	(3,602)	(3,335)
Other	(12,960)	(12,000)
Total cash paid for general and administrative activities	*(631,519)*	*(544,919)*
Cash flow before other operating activities	*358,657*	*331,388*
Cash from other operating activities		
Disposal of property, plant and equipment	37,650	-
Investment in associate A	-	(120,000)
Sale of receivable	8,000	10,000
Settlement of cash flow hedge	3,402	3,150
Total cash received (paid) for other operating activities	*49,052*	*(106,850)*
Net cash from operating activities	**407,709**	**224,538**

	For the year ended 31 December	
	2010	**2009**
Investing		
Purchase of available-for-sale financial assets	-	(130,000)
Sale of available-for-sale financial assets	56,100	51,000
Dividends received	54,000	50,000
Net cash from investing activities	**110,100**	**(29,000)**
NET CASH FROM BUSINESS ACTIVITIES	**517,809**	**195,538**
FINANCING		
Interest received on cash	8,619	5,500
Total cash from financing assets	**8,619**	**5,500**
Proceeds from issue of short-term debt	162,000	150,000
Proceeds from issue of long-term debt	-	250,000
Interest paid	(83,514)	(82,688)
Dividends paid	(86,400)	(80,000)
Total cash from financing liabilities	**(7,914)**	**237,312**
NET CASH FROM FINANCING ACTIVITIES	**705**	**242,812**
Change in cash from continuing operations before taxes and equity	*518,514*	*438,350*
INCOME TAXES		
Cash taxes paid	(281,221)	(193,786)
Change in cash before discontinued operations and equity	*237,293*	*244,564*
DISCONTINUED OPERATIONS		
Cash paid from discontinued operations	(12,582)	(11,650)
NET CASH FROM DISCONTINUED OPERATIONS	**(12,582)**	**(11,650)**
Change in cash before equity	*224,711*	*232,914*
EQUITY		
Proceeds from reissue of treasury stock	84,240	78,000
NET CASH FROM EQUITY	**84,240**	**78,000**
Effect of foreign exchange rates on cash	3,209	1,027
CHANGE IN CASH	**312,161**	**311,941**
Beginning cash	**861,941**	**550,000**
Ending cash	**1,174,102**	**861,941**

Source: IASB, *Preliminary Views on Financial Statement Presentation,* October 2008.

Exhibit 4: ToolCo Financial Statements (Proposed Format)
STATEMENT OF CHANGES IN EQUITY

	Share capital	Retained earnings	Foreign currency translation adjustment—consolidated subsidiary	Foreign currency translation adjustment—associate A	Revaluation surplus	Unrealized gain on cash flow hedge	Unrealized gain on available-for-sale financial assets	Total equity
Balance at 31 Dec. 2008	1,265,000	280,250	50,200	37,000	800	31,000	6,000	1,670,250
Issue of share capital	78,000							78,000
Dividends		(80,000)						(80,000)
Total comprehensive income		448,039	(1,492)	(1,300)	-	1,690	15,275	462,212
Balance at 31 Dec. 2009	1,343,000	648,289	48,708	35,700	800	32,690	21,275	2,130,462
Issue of share capital	84,240							84,240
Dividends		(86,400)						(86,400)
Total comprehensive income		538,469	2,094	(1,404)	3,653	1,825	17,193	561,830
Balance at 31 Dec. 2010	1,427,240	1,100,358	50,802	34,296	4,453	34,515	38,468	2,690,132

Source: IASB, *Preliminary Views on Financial Statement Presentation*, October 2008.

Exhibit 5: ToolCo Financial Statements (Proposed Format)

RECONCILIATION OF CASH FLOWS TO COMPREHENSIVE INCOME

For the year ended 31 December 2009

	A	B	C	D	E	F	G
		Changes in Assets and Liabilities, Excluding Transactions with Owners				Statement of Comprehensive Income	
		Not from Remeasurements		From Remeasurements			
	Caption in Statement of Cash Flows	Cash Flows	Accruals, Allocations, and Other	Recurring Valuation Adjustments	All Other	Comprehensive Income (B + C + D + E)	Caption in Statement of Comprehensive Income
	BUSINESS **Operating**						**BUSINESS** **Operating**
	Cash received from wholesale customers	1,928,798	662,602			2,591,400	Sales—wholesale
	Cash received from retail customers	643,275	4,575			647,850	Sales—retail
	Total cash collected from customers	*2,572,073*	*667,177*			*3,239,250*	*Total revenue*
	Cash paid for goods						Cost of goods sold
	Materials purchases	(785,000)	(140,000)			(925,000)	Materials
	Labour	(475,313)	25,313			(450,000)	Labour
	Pension	(157,500)	104,250	6,000		(47,250)	Pension
			(215,000)			(215,000)	Overhead—depreciation
	Overhead—transport	(108,000)				(108,000)	Overhead—transport
	Overhead—other	(27,000)				(27,000)	Overhead—other
							Change in inventory
			(46,853)		9,500)	(46,853)	Loss on obsolete and damaged inventory
						(9,500)	

(Continued)

Exhibit 5: ToolCo Financial Statements (Proposed Format) (*Continued*)

RECONCILIATION OF CASH FLOWS TO COMPREHENSIVE INCOME

For the year ended 31 December 2009

A	B	C	D	E	F	G
	Changes in Assets and Liabilities, Excluding Transactions with Owners				**Statement of Comprehensive Income**	
	Not from Remeasurements		**From Remeasurements**			
Caption in Statement of Cash Flows	**Cash Flows**	**Accruals, Allocations, and Other**	**Recurring Valuation Adjustments**	**All Other**	**Comprehensive Income (B + C + D + E)**	**Caption in Statement of Comprehensive Income**
Total cash paid for selling activities	*(142,953)*	*12,919*			*(130,034)*	*Total selling expenses*
Cash paid for general and administrative activities						General and administrative expenses
Wages, salaries, and benefits	(314,234)	16,734			(297,500)	Wages, salaries, and benefits
Contributions to pension plan	(157,500)	104,250	6,000		(47,250)	Pension
Capital expenditures	(50,000)	50,000				
		(58,500)			(58,500)	Depreciation
Settlement of share-based remuneration	(3,335)	(8,665)	(5,000)		(17,000)	Share-based remuneration
Lease payments		(16,500)			(16,500)	Interest on lease liability
Research and development	(7,850)				(7,850)	Research and development
Other	(12,000)	(2,600)			(14,600)	Other
Total cash paid for general and admin. activities	*(544,919)*	*84,719*	*1,000*		*(459,200)*	*Total general and administrative expenses*

Income statement item						Cash flow item
Income before other operating items	*821,413*	*(9,500)*	*7,000*	*492,525*	*331,388*	*Cash flow before other operating activities*
Other operating income (expense)						Cash from other operating activities
Share of profit of associate A	22,000	22,000		120,000	(120,000)	Investment in associate A
Loss on sale of receivable	(2,025)	(2,025)		(10,000)	10,000	Sale of receivable
Realized gain on cash flow hedge	3,700		1,100	(550)	3,150	Settlement of cash flow hedge
Impairment loss on goodwill	(35,033)	(35,033)				
Total other operating income	*(11,358)*	*(15,058)*	*1,100*	*109,450*	*(106,850)*	*Total cash paid for other operating activities*
Total operating income	**810,055**	**(24,558)**	**8,100**	**601,975**	**224,538**	**Net cash from operating activities**
Investing						Investing
Realized gain on available-for-sale financial assets	7,500			130,000	(130,000)	Purchase of available-for-sale financial assets
Dividend income	50,000			(43,500)	51,000	Sale of available-for-sale financial assets
Share of profit of associate B	3,250	3,250			50,000	Dividends received
Total investing income	**60,750**	**3,250**		**86,500**	**(29,000)**	**Net cash from investing activities**
TOTAL BUSINESS INCOME	**870,805**	**(21,308)**	**8,100**	**688,475**	**195,538**	**NET CASH FROM BUSINESS ACTIVITIES**

(Continued)

Exhibit 5: ToolCo Financial Statements (Proposed Format) (*Continued*)

RECONCILIATION OF CASH FLOWS TO COMPREHENSIVE INCOME

For the year ended 31 December 2009

A	B	C	D	E	F	G
		Changes in Assets and Liabilities, Excluding Transactions with Owners			**Statement of Comprehensive Income**	
	Not from Remeasurements		From Remeasurements			
Caption in Statement of Cash Flows	Cash Flows	Accruals, Allocations, and Other	Recurring Valuation Adjustments	All Other	Comprehensive Income (B + C + D + E)	**Caption in Statement of Comprehensive Income**
FINANCING Interest received on cash	5,500				5,500	**FINANCING** Interest income on cash
Total cash from financing assets	**5,500**				**5,500**	Total financing asset income
Proceeds from issue of short-term debt	150,000	(150,000)				
Proceeds from issue of long-term debt	250,000	(250,000)				
Interest paid	(82,688)	(27,563)			(110,250)	Interest expense
Dividends paid	(80,000)	80,000				
Total cash from financing liabilities	**237,312**	**(347,563)**			**(110,250)**	**Total financing liability expense**
NET CASH FROM FINANCING ACTIVITIES	**242,812**	**(347,563)**			**104,750**	**TOTAL NET FINANCING EXPENSE**
Change in cash from continuing operations before taxes and equity	*438,350*	*340,912*	*8,100*	*(21,308)*	*766,055*	*Profit from continuing operations before taxes and other comprehensive income*

Comprehensive income statement

INCOME TAXES			
Income tax expense	(295,266)	(21,308)	
Net profit from continuing operations	*470,789*		*8,100*
DISCONTINUED OPERATIONS			
Loss on discontinued operations	(35,000)	(23,350)	
Tax benefit	12,250		
NET LOSS FROM DISCONTINUED OPERATIONS	**(22,750)**	**(23,350)**	
NET PROFIT	**448,039**	**(44,658)**	**8,100**
OTHER COMPREHENSIVE INCOME (after tax)			
Unrealized gain on available-for-sale securities	15,275		15,275
Unrealized gain on cash flow hedge	1,690		1,690
Foreign currency translation adjust—consolidated sub.	(1,492)	(1,492)	
Foreign currency translation adjust—associate A	(1,300)	(1,300)	
TOTAL OTHER COMPREHENSIVE INCOME	**14,173**	**(2,792)**	**16,965**
TOTAL COMPREHENSIVE INCOME	**462,212**	**(47,450)**	**25,065**

Cash flow statement

INCOME TAXES		
Cash taxes paid	(101,480)	(193,786)
Change in cash before discontinued operations and equity	*239,432*	*244,564*
DISCONTINUED OPERATIONS		
Cash paid from discontinued operations	12,250	(11,650)
NET CASH FROM DISCONTINUED OPERATIONS	**12,250**	**(11,650)**
Change in cash before equity	**251,682**	**232,914**
Change in cash before equity	**251,682**	**232,914**

Source: IASB, *Preliminary Views on Financial Statement Presentation*, October 2008.

1. What are IFRS and how do they relate to IAS?
2. What is the objective of financial statements and what two assumptions underlie them?
3. Why are qualitative characteristics important?
4. What is the difference between understandability and relevance?
5. Is reliability the same as accuracy?
6. What are the characteristics of reliability?
7. What is comparability and to what does it apply?
8. List the five sections that all proposed financial statements should contain.
9. How does the balance sheet under proposed IFRS differ from U.S. GAAP?
10. What is the proposed new name for the income statement and why does it have this name?
11. How does the proposed IFRS statement of cash flows differ from the way most of these statements are prepared in the United States?
12. What does the proposed schedule in Exhibit 5 reconcile and why is it useful?
13. *Class or group discussion*: Is historical cost or fair value more in line with the qualitative characteristics of the conceptual framework and why?
14. *Class or group discussion*: Define the concepts of *conservatism* under U.S. GAAP and *prudence* under IFRS. How are they similar and how are they different? Do they represent a significant difference between U.S. GAAP and IFRS? Give an example of how they might differ in their application.
15. *Exercise*: Match the selected sections of IASB-proposed financial statements (letters) with their respective components (numbers):
    a. Statement of comprehensive income—business
    b. Statement of comprehensive income—financing
    c. Statement of financial position—business
    d. Statement of financial position—financing
    e. Statement of cash flows—business
    f. Statement of cash flows—financing
    g. None of the above
        1. Operating cash flows
        2. Financing assets
        3. Discontinued operations
        4. Financing liability expense
        5. Operating income and expense
        6. Investing cash flows
        7. Financing liability cash flows
        8. Investing assets and liabilities
        9. Financing liabilities
        10. Financing asset income
        11. Financing asset cash flows
        12. Operating assets and liabilities
        13. Income taxes
        14. Investing income and expense

III. KEY DIFFERENCES BETWEEN IFRS AND U.S. GAAP

Differences between U.S. GAAP and IFRS are numerous. Several years ago the FASB published *The IASC-US Comparison Project*. Literally hundreds of differences were identified in it.[1] Many differences were minor technicalities but some were major. The volume provides evidence of the problem's scope and eventually led to the convergence efforts of the IASB and the FASB. Underlying reasons for these differences exist. This section summarizes several major differences between IFRS and U.S. GAAP.

PRINCIPLES-BASED VERSUS RULES-BASED STANDARDS

Considerable debate exists regarding the issue of principles-based versus rules-based standards. *Rules-based standards* are perceived to be the dominant approach of the FASB. This approach attempts to anticipate all or most of the application issues and prescribes solutions. *Principles-based standards* are stated as the dominant approach of the IASB. In this case, the standards are less prescriptive and rely on broad statements of objectives and principles to be followed. Greater reliance is placed on the preparer's judgment to align the financial reporting with the conceptual framework.

Perceived differences in the two approaches are shown in Table 2. Proponents of the FASB approach argue that the standards are rooted in the conceptual framework and that preparers demand guidance in specific situations. U.S. GAAP is older than IFRS and over time has developed a detailed prescription. In time, the IASB will face pressure from preparers and auditors to provide more guidance. Critics of rules-based standards argue that companies structure agreements and transactions to achieve particular objectives and may not reflect the underlying substance. For example, companies structure long-term lease agreements as operating leases when in substance they are capital leases. The result is significant "off-the-balance-sheet" financing. Proponents of principle-based standards argue that they also contain rules and it is only a matter of degree. More importantly in the case of long-term leases, the lease would be judged as a capital lease regardless of the specific terms resulting in greater comparability because like items would be treated in a similar way. There is no doubt that principles-based standards place more reliance on professional judgment. However, judgments are often dependent on the person's culture and prior experience. For instance, research shows that a preparer's judgment often falls back on the historical practices of his/her country, which may differ from past practices in another country. Thus, judgments often differ from person to person, company to company, and industry to industry.

INCOME MEASUREMENT

Both U.S. GAAP and IFRS recognize accrual accounting as the key concept underlying income measurement. However, the FASB and IASB implement this concept very differently, as shown in Figure 3. U.S. GAAP emphasizes the matching rule and measurement of items on the income

---

[1] Carrier Bloomer, ed., *The IASC-US Comparison Project: A Report on the Similarities and Differences between IASC Standards and U.S. GAAP* (Norwalk, Conn.: FASB, 1996).

Table 2: Comparison of Rules-Based Standards and Principles-Based Standards

Attribute	Rules-Based Standards	Principles-Based Standards
Conceptual framework	Less reliance	More reliance
Professional judgment	Less reliance	More reliance
Level of detailed guidance	More	Less
Amount of industry specific guidance	Extensive	Little

statement. Thus, revenues are recognized in the periods earned and expenses are recorded in the periods in which they occurred. The balance sheet impacts—increases, decreases, or both in assets and liabilities—are the result from these recognitions of revenue and expense. However, IFRS measure assets and liabilities on the balance sheet at fair value with resulting increases, decreases, or both, which then are reflected as revenues and expenses in the income statement. In other words, revenues and expenses under IFRS are matched through a balance sheet valuation process.

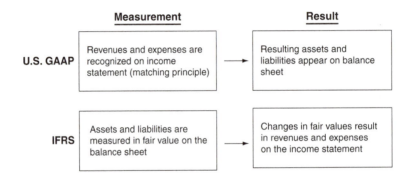

Figure 3: Contrasting Approaches To Accrual Accounting and Income Determination

FAIR VALUE MEASUREMENTS

In the IFRS approach to income measurement, the determination of fair value is critical. By contrast, various notions of value are also important under U.S. GAAP. For example, except for cash and land, assets are usually carried at either estimated or market value. However, U.S. GAAP has many definitions of market value. For instance, inventory is measured at lower of cost or market, where market is measured by replacement (or entry) cost. When receivables are estimated or valued at net of allowance for uncollectible accounts, the value is net realizable (exit) value. All long-term assets, except land, are subject to estimates of depreciation, depletion, or amortization and are subject to annual impairment tests, which can be based on various concepts of market depending on the situation. Securities (except held-to maturity) are valued at market price usually from an established market.

In contrast to U.S. GAAP, IASB defines fair value as a single concept based on exit value. Specifically, fair value is the amount an asset may be exchanged for, or a liability settled, between knowledgeable parties in an arm's length transaction. The best evidence of fair value is quoted prices in an active market. If the market for a financial instrument is not active, a valuation technique must be used. The objective of a valuation technique is to establish what the transaction price is on the measurement date in an arm's length exchange motivated by normal business considerations. Valuation techniques include using arm's length market transactions between knowledgeable, willing parties, if available; reference to the current fair value of another instrument that is substantially the same; discounted cash flow analysis; and options pricing models.[2]

REVENUE RECOGNITION

As discussed earlier, revenue recognition under U.S. GAAP and IFRS take different approaches. Under U.S. GAAP, revenue is defined without respect to the balance sheet effect. It must meet all the following conditions before revenue is to be recognized:[3]

- Persuasive evidence of an arrangement exists.
- Product or service has been delivered.
- Seller's price to the buyer is fixed or determinable.
- Collectability is reasonably assured.

By contrast, IFRS define revenue from a balance sheet point of view. Revenue is viewed as the gross inflow of economic benefits during the period arising in the course of the ordinary activities of an entity when the inflows result in an increase in equity (other than investments from investors). Revenue is measured as the fair value for which the asset could be exchanged, or the liability settled, between knowledgeable, willing parties to an arm's length transaction. IFRS go on to say that revenue is recognized when:

- There are probable future economic benefits.
- Revenue can be measured reliably.
- Costs can be measured reliably.
- Significant risk and rewards of ownership are transferred.
- Managerial involvement is not retained as to ownership or control.

While similar to U.S. GAAP criteria, the main difference is that future commitments would not be recognized under U.S. GAAP but may be recognized under IFRS if these criteria are met. For example, if a company has a firm commitment or agreement to provide services in the future at a fixed price, the above criteria may be met. It is possible to determine the future cash flows, and therefore the fair value, of the agreement. Thus, an asset exists and recognition occurs.

In applying these revenue recognition concepts, U.S. GAAP often relies on industry practice whereas IFRS rely more on judgment. U.S. GAAP addresses revenue recognition extensively in sixteen standards, twenty-four interpretations, and numerous other related documents. IFRS include two standards and three interpretations on the subject. For instance, IFRS typically record service revenue using the *percentage-of-completion method* (recognizing revenue as the percentage of the total project completed at each stage) whereas U.S. GAAP relies more on specific

---

[2] IASB Expert Advisory Panel, "Measuring and Disclosing the Fair Value of Financial Instruments in Markets that are No Longer Active," October 2008.
[3] Securities and Exchange Commission, *Staff Accounting Bulletin No. 10*, 1999.

industry guidance. For the software industry, U.S. GAAP provides specific guidance for typical software arrangements, upfront fees, and multiple deliverable arrangements whereas IFRS provide only general guidance. However, IFRS provide specific guidance for revenue recognition on construction contracts, requiring the use of percentage-of-completion method. Alternatively, U.S. GAAP allows either percentage of completion or the *completed-contract method* (recognizing all revenue at the time the contract is completed). For example, Boeing currently recognizes all revenue when an aircraft is delivered even though it takes more than a year to build it. But under IFRS, the company would recognize revenue at each stage of building the aircraft.

PROVISIONS

U.S. GAAP does not record commitments, such as purchase agreements, as liabilities even though they are a legal obligation since they do not meet the technical definition of a liability. Disclosure in a note to the financial statements is required. Under IFRS, these agreements are recognized when an entity has a demonstrable commitment.

COMPREHENSIVE INCOME AND RECYCLING

Remember, entities are required to present either a combined statement of comprehensive income or two separate statements—one for profit and loss and one for other comprehensive income. However, U.S. GAAP permits a firm to select from three reporting alternatives for comprehensive income—(1) a separate statement, (2) inclusion in the income statement, or (3) inclusion in the statement of stockholders' equity. Currently, 80 percent of U.S. companies follow the latter approach,[4] but under IFRS only the first two approaches are allowed. Also, U.S. GAAP and IFRS are similar in that items included in comprehensive income may be reported net of tax.

Recycling occurs if an item, such as an unrealized gain and loss, is previously classified as other comprehensive income and later is realized in net income. Under IFRS and U.S. GAAP recycling occurs for the following items:

- Cumulative foreign currency translation adjustments
- Unrealized gains and losses on AFS securities
- Unrealized gains and losses on effective cash flow hedges

Actuarial gains and losses are recycled under U.S. GAAP, but IFRS recognize the OCI amount immediately in retained earnings. Finally, IFRS forbid recycling of revaluation surplus associated with long-lived assets (see discussion below).

INVENTORY ACCOUNTING

Inventory accounting is essentially the same with two major exceptions. First, IFRS specifically forbid the use of LIFO (last in, first out), a method of accounting for the cost of inventory. LIFO is used by more than one-third of U.S. companies[5] because in periods of rising

---

[4] American Institute of CPAs, *Accounting Trends and Techniques* (New York: 62nd edition, 2008), p. 430.
[5] American Institute of CPAs, *Accounting Trends and Techniques* (New York: 62nd edition, 2008), p. 159.

prices, it produces a lower taxable income. The U.S. income tax law requires the use of LIFO for financial reporting purposes *if* a company uses LIFO for tax purposes. Prohibiting LIFO for financial reporting purposes could be a barrier to U.S. adoption of IFRS. The LIFO companies would recognize potentially large taxable gains on inventory valuation if they were forced to change from LIFO to another method. However, a change in the tax law permitting LIFO for tax purposes without mandating its use for financial reporting would eliminate this barrier.

Second, U.S. GAAP values inventory using the lower-of-cost-or-market method. This differs from IFRS in three ways. First, market is defined as net replacement value, not fair value as defined by IFRS; second, U.S. GAAP does not recognize increases in market above cost but IFRS do; and, third, U.S. GAAP prohibits the reversal of write downs if replacement costs subsequently increases but IFRS does not.

PROPERTY, PLANT, AND EQUIPMENT REVALUATION

Three major differences between U.S. GAAP and IFRS in the accounting for property, plant, and equipment (PPE) are:

- Revaluation
- Component depreciation
- Interest cost during construction

Revaluation recognizes a change in the fair value of an asset after its initial acquisition. U.S. GAAP does not allow revaluation except for financial instruments and business combinations. IFRS, on the other hand, *permit* revaluation for tangible and identifiable long-term assets (including PPE) and *require* it for investment properties and for agricultural products. In the latter two cases, the change in fair value is reported on the income statement. Under U.S. GAAP, PPE must be carried at historical cost less accumulated depreciation. By contrast, IFRS allow PPE to be valued at historical cost or at fair value if readily measurable less accumulated depreciation.

IFRS require depreciation of assets on a component basis, U.S. GAAP does not. The component basis acknowledges that each component of a building, production process, or other PPE asset has its own useful life and fair value. Finally, U.S. GAAP requires interest cost on assets during contraction to be capitalized as a part of PPE and depreciated, whereas IFRS allow expensing or capitalization. Interest cost on constructed assets is now included as part of the convergence project.

When electing to revalue, the revaluation must be applied to the entire class or component of PPE, such as land, buildings, or equipment. When revaluation results in an increase a debit is made to the asset account and a credit is made to an equity account called *revaluation surplus*. When a revaluation results in a decrease to an asset, a debit is made to a loss account (or a previously established revaluation surplus) and a credit is made to an asset account.

To illustrate, assume that in 2009 Turnbow Company measures property, plant, and equipment at revalued amounts and that it owns a building with a cost of $100,000 and a current fair value of $120,000. The increase from the cost of the building to its fair value follows:

2010:

Building	20,000	
Revaluation Surplus, Building		20,000

After revaluation, the value on the balance sheet must represent its current fair value. At each year end, management should consider whether the asset's fair value materially differs from its carrying value.

Subsequent decreases in an asset's value are first charged against any previous revaluation surplus for that asset; then, the excess should be expensed. If previous revaluations resulted in an expense, subsequent increases in value should be charged to income to the extent of the previous expense. Any excess is credited to equity (revaluation surplus).

Next, assume that in 2011 Turnbow Company determines that the fair value of the building has decreased to $90,000. The appropriate entry is as follows:

2011:

Revaluation Surplus, Buildings	20,000	
Revaluation Loss, Buildings	10,000	
Buildings		30,000

After a revaluation, accumulated depreciation must be also remeasured. Two methods are permitted as follows:

- Accumulated depreciation is restated proportionately so that the asset's carrying amount after revaluation equals its revalued amount.
- Accumulated depreciation is eliminated against the asset's gross carrying amount and the net amount is restated to the revalued amount of the asset.

To illustrate the first method, assume that Turnbow Company owns a different building that costs $200,000 with accumulated depreciation of $80,000 and a carrying value of $120,000. Assume the building's current fair value is $150,000. Turnbow restates both the building account and the accumulated depreciation account using the ratio of net carrying amount to gross carrying amount of 80% (120,000/150,000). The building's carrying value is increased to the fair value in the following entry, which increases the Building to $250,000, Accumulated Depreciation to $100,000, Carrying Value to $150,000, and creates a Revaluation Surplus of $30,000:

Building	50,000	
Accumulated Depreciation, building		20,000
Revaluation Surplus, Building		30,000
$200,000/.8 = $150,000; $200,000 − $150,000 = $50,000		
$80,000/.8 = $100,000; $100,000 − $ 80,000 = $20,000		

Under the second method, Turnbow first reduces accumulated depreciation by $80,000 to $0. Next, the resulting balance of the buildings account of $120,000 ($200,000 − 80,000) increased by $30,000 and now the carrying value equals the $150,000 fair value. The entries are as follows:

Accumulated Depreciation, Buildings	80,000	
Buildings		80,000
Buildings	30,000	
Revaluation Surplus, Buildings		30,000

In both cases, the resulting carrying value of the Building is increased to $150,000 and a revaluation surplus of $30,000 is recorded. Next year, the annual depreciation expense will be based on the $150,000 carrying value. In addition the buildings will be assessed for revaluation in subsequent years. At derecognition date, any remaining revaluation surplus is closed directly to retained earnings.

The revaluation surplus included in equity may be transferred directly to retained earnings when the surplus is realized, such as in the case of sale of the asset. It may also be realized over time as the asset is used by the entity. Also, subsequent depreciation is applied to the remaining carrying value of the building. Thus, assuming the building has a remaining useful life of 20 years and has no salvage value, depreciation will be computed on the carrying value of the building at $150,000, resulting in annual depreciation of $7,500 ($150,000/20 years). The realized revaluation surplus will be realized annually in the amount of $2,500 ($50,000/20 years). The entry is as follows:

Depreciation Expense	7,500	
Revaluation Surplus, Building	2,500	
Accumulated Depreciation, Buildings		7,500
Retained Earnings		2,500

The revaluation surplus, assuming no further revaluations (or impairments), will reduce to 0 over the 20-year period.

IMPAIRMENT

While both U.S. GAAP and IFRS provide for impairment testing of long-lived assets (tangible and intangible), the differences are significant. U.S. GAAP requires impairment tests at the "reporting unit" (RU) level whereas IFRS test for impairment at the "cash generating unit" (CGU) level. The RU is an operating unit, or one-step below an operating unit, for which management regularly reviews financial information. ACGU is the smallest identifiable group of assets that generates cash inflows that are largely independent of the cash inflows of other assets or groups of assets. In some companies, these approaches may result in different units to which impairment tests are applied, and therefore produce different results. How to test also differs.

U.S. GAAP impairment tests for long-lived assets are a two-step process:

1. If the total undiscounted future cash flows of RU long-lived assets is greater than their carrying value, then no impairment exists and no further step is required.
2. If the carrying value of their assets is less than the total undiscounted future cash flows (present value), then compute the present value of the future cash flows. The impairment loss equals the carrying value minus the discounted cash flows.

IFRS impairment tests do not consider undiscounted cash flows, but compare the carrying value with the recoverable amount which is the greater of

- Net selling price—the market value of the asset less disposal costs.
- Value in use—the discounted value of the future net cash flows (present value).

Furthermore, U.S. GAAP prohibits impairment reversals in the future, but IFRS allow such reversals if values recover except for goodwill that cannot be reversed.

To illustrate IFRS treatment, consider a building with a fair value of $180,000 and a carrying value of $224,000. The asset impairment of $44,000 ($224,000 – $180,000) is recorded as follows:

Impairment Loss (expense)	$44,000	
Accumulated Impairment Loss		$44,000

If the impaired asset was revalued at any time, the impairment loss would first result in a reversal of the revaluation surplus and any deficit would be charged to the income statement.

Assume a building with a revaluation surplus of $25,000 was deemed impaired by $39,000. The entry to record the asset at fair value is:

Impairment Loss	$14,000	
Revaluation Surplus. Building	25,000	
Accumulated Impairment Loss		$14,000
Building		25,000

In either case, if a reversal of fair value occurs then accumulated impairment loss is reversed and reported in the income statement.

RESEARCH AND DEVELOPMENT COSTS

Several important differences between U.S. GAAP and IFRS exist with regard to accounting for research and development costs. U.S. GAAP requires both research and development costs to be expensed as incurred. By contrast, IFRS require research costs to be expensed but development costs to be capitalized and amortized. Under IFRS, in-process research and development costs, acquired as part of a business combination, are capitalized, amortized, and are subject to impairment tests. For now, U.S. GAAP requires expensing of in-process research and development although this may change as part of the convergence project.

EQUITY

A major classification difference between U.S. GAAP and IFRS relates to 1) the definition of equity and 2) the distinction between debt and equity. Equity accounting is part of the convergence project, which will possibly reduce the difference.

Under IFRS, equity includes only the common or basic shareholder interests, whereas under U.S. GAAP stockholders' equity includes all shareholder interest including preferred stock. The terminology is also different as shown in Table 3.

Table 3: Equity Terminology under U.S. GAAP and IFRS

U.S. GAAP	IFRS
Common stock	Share capital
Paid-in capital or	
Additional paid-in capital	Share premium
Retained earnings or	Retained earnings, retained profits, or
Reinvested earnings	Accumulated profit and loss
Treasury stock	Treasury stock
Accumulated other comprehensive income	General reserves or other reserve accounts

"Reserves" is a term rarely used in U.S. GAAP, but is often used in IFRS to refer to all equity accounts other than share capital and premium. General reserves include components of other comprehensive income. Revaluation surplus is classified in equity as other reserve accounts.

Treasury stock is shown as a deduction in both cases but under IFRS it may be deducted against any of the equity accounts on the basis of judgment as to the most appropriate account. No gains or losses are recorded on sale on treasury. Any difference between purchase and sale price is an increase or decrease in equity.

Under U.S. GAAP, there is a "mezzanine" category, which exists between debt and equity. Examples of this mezzanine level are deferred income taxes and minority interest. IFRS, on the other hand, do not recognize this "neither debt nor equity" category. Under IFRS everything is either debt or equity and equity is limited to the common stockholder interest. This raises questions in at least three areas:

- How are compound financial instruments such as convertible bonds and stocks, which have characteristics of both debt and equity, to be classified?
    - U.S. GAAP: convertible bonds are classified as debt and convertible stock is classified as equity.
    - IFRS: "split" accounting is required for these compound instruments. Under split accounting, the proceeds of the financial instrument are allocated between its debt component at fair value and it equity component at the residual value.
- How is minority interest classified?
    - U.S. GAAP: Minority interest is classified as "mezzanine" and thus is not part of equity.
    - IFRS: Minority interest is classified as equity.
- How should deferred income tax assets and liabilities be classified?
    - U.S. GAAP: Deferred income tax assets and liabilities are classified based on the classification of the related asset or liability. Thus, the classification may be either current or non-current.
    - IFRS: Deferred income tax assets **or** liabilities are classified only as non-current.

SHARE-BASED PAYMENTS

U.S. GAAP and IFRS handle share-based payments (SBP) in a similar manner in that both:

- Recognize goods or services paid in shares or SBP.
- Measure SBP at fair value on the grant date.
- True up for failure to meet service, non-market vesting conditions.
- Do not true up for failure to meet market conditions.
- Remeasure cash-settled SBP through settlement.

A major difference is that U.S. GAAP rules apply only to employee SBP, whereas IFRS apply to all SBP, including non-employee SBP. Numerous other technical differences are beyond the current discussion.

CONSOLIDATION

U.S. GAAP, with few exceptions, requires a greater than 50 percent ownership before financial statements of related companies are consolidated into a single set of financial statements. IFRS place more weight on judgment rather than voting control. IFRS consolidation is based on assessing risks and rewards, as well as governance and decision-making activities.

Thus, under IFRS, consolidation may be required more often than under U.S. GAAP when a company has less than 50 percent ownership but effectively controls the other entity. Consequently, joint ventures, special purpose entities (SPE), and franchises will more likely be consolidated.

Beginning in 2009, both U.S. GAAP and IFRS will report income of less than 100 percent owned subsidiaries in the same way. The parent company will include 100 percent of the subsidiary's income in its income. The income attributable to shareholders of the subsidiary will be deducted on the face of the statements to present net income attributable to the parent.

IFRS FOR PRIVATE ENTITIES

For several years the issue of separate accounting standards for private entities (previously referred to as small- and medium-sized entities (SMEs) has received much scrutiny. Should private entities (PE) be allowed certain exemptions or other concessions when adopting IFRS? Millions of entities are potentially impacted. Currently, lack of comparability is widespread among these entities because of different national practices. Almost every European country has developed its own simplified national GAAP for private entities. Some countries have two or three levels of standards for these entities. The same is true in Asia and elsewhere. In response, the IASB initiated a project "to develop International Financial Reporting Standards (IFRS) expressly designed to meet the financial reporting needs of entities that (a) do not have public accountability and (b) publish general purpose financial statements for external users."[6] In 2007, the IASB released an exposure draft and subsequently considered the numerous comments received. The new, simpler IFRS for private entities are expected to be released in the first quarter 2009. Once issued, voluntary or mandated adoption of IFRS for PE will be determined on a country-by-country basis.

REVIEW QUESTIONS

1. What are rules-based and principles-based standards and how do they differ in application across four characteristics?
2. How do U.S. GAAP and IFRS differ in their implementation of accrual accounting?
3. Why is fair value critical to U.S. GAAP and IFRS and how do they differ in the application of fair value?
4. Why is revenue recognition a good example of the contrasting approaches of IFRS and U.S. GAAP to level of detail?
5. How does the IFRS balance sheet approach to revenue recognition differ for the U.S. GAAP approach?
6. Do U.S. GAAP or IFRS give more industry guidance? Give an example.
7. How do U.S. GAAP and IFRS differ with regard to recognition of purchase commitments?
8. What is recycling and how does it apply to comprehensive income?

---

[6] International Accounting Standards Board, "International Financial Reporting Standard for Private Entities," IASCF (August 1, 2008), 1.

9. What are the two main differences in inventory accounting between U.S. GAAP and IFRS?
10. What are the three major differences between U.S. GAAP and IFRS?
11. What is revaluation; to what does it apply; and how would it result in a revaluation surplus? Where does the revaluation surplus appear in the financial statements?
12. What are the two methods that may be used to accomplish a revaluation?
13. What eventually happens to the revaluation surplus?
14. To what business units does impairment test apply under U.S. GAAP and IFRS?
15. How do impairment tests differ under U.S. GAAP and IFRS?
16. What is the difference in accounting for research and development cost between U.S. GAAP and IFRS?
17. What is a mezzanine category and why is it an important classification issue?
18. How does the classification of minority interests, deferred tax and liabilities, and convertible bonds and stocks differ under U.S. GAAP and IFRS?
19. What role does judgment play in deciding whether a controlling interest exists for consolidation under U.S. GAAP and IFRS?
20. What is the expectation with regard to IFRS for private entities?
21. *Discussion or group question*: Among the differences between U.S. GAAP and IFRS listed in this section, which two do you feel the most difficult to reconcile and why?
22. *Exercise: Revaluation*

Reval Inc. prepares financial statements in accordance with IFRS and has elected to use the revaluation model in IAS 16 to account for its buildings. Reval Inc. acquired a building on January 1, 20X1 for $300,000. At that time it estimated the useful life of the building to be 60 years, with no residual value. It is now January 1, 20X8. The carrying amount of the building is $275,000 ($300,000 − (5 × $5,000)). Reval Inc. has obtained an appraisal valuing the building at $385,000.

Part I:

1. Show the accounting entries to recognize the revaluation and corresponding depreciation in 20X8.
2. Show the balances on the building and revaluation surplus accounts at December 31, 20X8.

Part II:

On January 1, 20X9, a major fire damages a significant part of the building. Reval Inc. has no insurance and the value of the damaged building is impaired, such that the remainder of the building has a value of only $250,000. Show the entries to reflect the impairment on 1.1.20X9.

23. *Exercise: Impairment*

Impair Inc. has an operating segment that is composed of three cash generating units (CGUs) as follows:

CGU A – retail operations located in the Midwestern U.S.
CGU B – retail operations located in the Eastern U.S.
CGU C – retail operations located in the Pacific Northwest U.S.

Impair has discrete financial information available for each CGU, however segment management does not regularly review the operating results of each CGU. Financial information for each CGU is as follows:

	CGU A	CGU B	CGU C
Identifiable long-lived assets	100,000	250,000	250,000
Other identifiable net assets	25,000	20,000	50,000
Goodwill	75,000	50,000	80,000
Book value	200,000	320,000	380,000
Undiscounted cash flows of CGU	225,000	225,000	700,000
Value in use of CGU	190,000	190,000	570,000
Fair value of CGU	185,000	185,000	560,000

The fair value of the operating segment (CGUs A, B, and C collectively) is 940,000.

Under IFRS:

1. Determine the amount of impairment loss to be recognized and the amount of any impairment loss that is assigned to goodwill.

2. Determine what amount, if any, of the impairment loss potentially is available to recover if the situation changes at a later point in time.

Under U.S. GAAP:

1. Determine the amount of impairment loss to be recognized and the amount of any impairment loss that is assigned to goodwill.

2. Determine what amount, if any, of the impairment loss is potentially available to recover if the situation changes at a later point in time.

IV. THE CURRENT STATUS AND FUTURE OF IFRS

The momentum toward IFRS in the United States and elsewhere seems strong. The FASB, IASB, SEC, AICPA, big accounting firms, and others support this movement. The SEC road-map adds momentum to the potential adoption of IFRS for U.S. public companies. However, the change in administration in Washington and the economic uncertainty may slow the transition. Mary Schapiro, President Obama's choice as chair of the SEC, could delay the transition. Before the Senate Banking Committee, she said she will proceed with "great caution" and that she has "some concerns about the IFRS standards generally... not being as detailed as U.S. standards."[1] Some important accounting organizations including the National Association of State Boards of accountancy (NASBA)[2] and the New York Society of CPAs have opposed the SEC roadmap.[3] One prominent member of the Public Companies Accounting Oversight Board (PCAOB) has stated, "the switch to IFRS by 2014 could squander comparability among U.S. financial statements and impede the ability of regulators and auditors to do their jobs."[4]

However, a recent survey of accounting professionals by the AICPA taken after the SEC's latest roadmap shows the sentiment in business moving toward IFRS:

- 55 percent majority of CPAs at firms and companies nationwide are preparing in some way for adoption of IFRS (up from previous 41 percent previously).
- 45 percent are not preparing yet for IFRS (down from 59 percent previously).[5]

More recently, the Chair of the IASB, Sir David Tweedie, came to Washington to meet with Schapiro in an attempt to get the roadmap on track.[6]

Critics make valid points, but for such critics to prevail seems unlikely at present. Whatever the final timing of the SEC roadmap, the FASB/IASB convergence efforts and joint standards are closing the gap between U.S. GAAP and IFRS and companies are planning for the transition.

REMAINING DIFFERENCES BETWEEN U.S. GAAP AND IFRS

In sum, many similarities between U.S. GAAP and IFRS exist, and significant differences remain, including different:

- *Concepts and approaches*: for example, IFRS allow revaluation of non-financial assets
- *Acceptable methods*: for example, IFRS prohibit LIFO inventory accounting
- *Levels of details*: for example, the contrasting approaches to revenue recognition
- *Industry specific guidance*: for example, U.S. GAAP provides substantially more industry guidance

---

[1] "New SEC Chair May Delay IFRS Roadmap," *WebCPA*, January 16, 2009.

[2] "NASBA Response to SEC Roadmap," http://nasba.org, February 19, 2009.

[3] "New York CPAs Slam IFRS Roadmap," http://www.CFO.com, March 6, 2009.

[4] Quote attributed to Charles Niemeier in Penny Sukhraj "PCAOB Member Slams Stateside IFRS Plans," *Accountancy Age,* September 11, 2008.

[5] "U.S. CPAs Show Growing Acceptance of Change from U.S. to International Accounting Standards," AICPA Press Release (December 3, 2008).

[6] "IASB'S Tweedie Meets New SEC Chairman," http://www.Accountancyag.com, February 13, 2009.

- *Scope of application*: for example, employee share-based payments under U.S. GAAP versus all share-based payments under IFRS
- *Implementation details*: for example, differences in effective dates and transition

Over time as the joint IASB/FASB efforts continue, many differences will be reduced or eliminated. The IASB and FASB are collaborating on the many topics including:

- Consolidation
- Deregulation
- Emissions trading schemes
- Fair value measurement
- Financial instruments with characteristics of equity
- Financial Statement presentation
- Income taxes
- Insurance contracts
- Leases
- Post-employment benefits (including pensions)
- Revenue recognition
- Discontinued operations
- Earnings per share
- Various aspects of the conceptual framework[7]

TRANSITIONING TO IFRS

European companies have undergone the transition from their GAAP to IFRS since 2005, and thus provide some evidence as to how difficult the transition may be in the United States. Further, as noted previously, the SEC intends to see how difficult this transition will be in the United States by seeking volunteers to make the transition themselves by 2010. The IASB provides in IFRS No. 1 directions for first-time adopters to make this transition to IFRS.[8] For instance, when a company issues comparative financial statements, IFRS must be applied to the current year and retroactively to the prior year. While the IASB makes some allowances under IFRS No. 1 to facilitate the transition process, such as allowing for financial statement presentations that do not go as far as the proposed presentations discussed in Part 2 of this document, the transition to IFRS is quite technical, requires careful planning, and is likely to be more costly than experienced in Europe.[9]

Specific guidance is provided in IFRS No. 1 with regard to allowed exemptions by first-time adopters. For example, exemptions may be elected in some of the more complex reporting areas, such as other assets and liabilities, employee benefits, accumulated translation differences, compound financial instruments, insurance contracts, leases, and others. Also, companies may elect not to apply in the first year with certain fair value requirements in such areas as business combinations, revaluations, investment properties, and intangible assets. Estimates under IFRS should be consistent with those under U.S. GAAP unless there is objective evidence that those estimates were in error.

---

[7] "IASB Work Plan—Projected Timetable as of 31 October 2008," IASB, 2008.

[8] International Accounting Standards Board (IASB), *IFRS No. 1: First-Time Adoption of International Financial Reporting Standards*, IASB, 2007.

[9] Sarah Johnson, "Guessing the Cost of Conversion," http:www.CFO.com (March 30, 2009).

Finally, the company should provide a reconciliation with its IFRS financial statements to explain how the transition from U.S. GAAP to IFRS affected its reported financial position, financial performance, and cash flows.

Conversion to IFRS will require a whole company effort beyond just the accounting function. Key activities that will lead to a company's successful conversion include:

- Establishment of a project management team that has direction, comprehensive planning, execution tactics, and monitoring.
- Development of a conversion timeline.
- Identification of the areas other than financial reporting that will be affected.
- Development of an IT strategy that modifies all systems related to the conversion.
- Implementation of effective training across the entire organization.
- Learning from experiences in Europe and other countries.
- Establishment of a communications plan.[10]

ADAPTING TO IFRS

Future changes in IFRS are expected as the IASB issues IFRS for Private Entities, the process of convergence continues, and the changing business environment demands it.

Adapting to IFRS requires attention and study for U.S. accounting, audit, and tax practitioners, as well as accounting educators and students. Keeping up with all the changes is a daunting but important task. More importantly, the emphasis in IFRS accounting will not be on memorization of rules. The dual analytical effect of transactions resulting from business decisions and changes in the environment must be understood, but bookkeeping techniques are not essential knowledge. IFRS require accounting students (and educators) to realize that virtually every number in financial statements:

- Results from judgment and estimates
- Has a basis in valuation and fair value
- Is rooted in the conceptual framework
- Is based on an application of a standard

And therefore they must learn:

- To make judgments in a world of uncertainty
- To apply a variety of valuation models
- To focus on underlying concepts and their application
- To research standards and interpretations

Although the financial crisis may impede the SEC's effort to persuade 110 of the largest companies to voluntarily adopt IFRS,[11] most authorities feel the adoption of IFRS in the United States is simply a matter of time. As mentioned in the introduction, the AICPA has already made it possible through its code of professional conduct for U.S. private (non-public) companies to adopt IFRS. A recent survey shows that AICPA members expect a shift to IFRS in the next three to five years.[12] Another survey reports that investment executives and analysts believe that

---

[10] Danita Osling, "Converting to IFRS," http://journalofaccountancy.com (January 8, 2009).

[11] "Survey of Financial Execs Reveals Challenges with IFRS," *Business Finance* (November 25, 2008); "SEC Hit with Barrage of IFRS Transition Complaints, *Financial Week/Reuters* (November 19, 2008).

[12] "AICPA Members Expect Shift to IFRS to Take 3 to 5 Years," CIO Today (November, 2008).

IFRS will make U.S. stocks more attractive to foreign investors and that most feel the SEC timeline is "about right." However, the same survey says that less than 20 percent of investors and analysts understand the implications of IFRS.[13] Three to five years is a relatively short period. Students entering universities and colleges now will likely face IFRS when they graduate. For them to be well educated in IFRS, accounting educators face the imperative task of adapting the accounting curriculum for IFRS.

REVIEW QUESTIONS

1. What are the major types of differences between U.S. GAAP and IFRS? Give an example of each.
2. What are the main generalizations that can be made about IFRS?
3. What are the characteristics of numbers in the financial statements under IFRS?
4. Do companies that adopt IFRS have to follow all the standards in the first year? What are some possible exceptions?
5. What changes will likely take place in accounting education as a result of IFRS?
6. *Research question*: Choose one topic listed on page 44 that is being jointly studied by the IASB and the FASB. Go to the websites listed in Appendix D. Find references to the topic on at least five sites and summarize in two pages the status of this issue.
7. *Class or group discussion*: What do you think will be the most challenging obstacle for a company moving to adopt IFRS?

---

[13] "KPMG Survey Favors IFRS Adoption," *WebCPA*, February 23, 2009.

APPENDIX A: COMMON ACRONYMS

AICPA	American Institute of CPAs
ASBJ	Accounting Standards Board of Japan
EC	European Commission
FASB	Financial Accounting Standards Board
G4+1	Standard setters in the United Kingdom, Canada, the United States, and Australia, plus the IASC
IFAC	International Federation of Accountants
IAAER	International Association for Accounting Education and Research
IASCF	IASC Foundation
IAS	International Accounting Standards
IFRIC	International Financial Reporting Interpretation Committee
IFRS	International Financial Reporting Standards
IASC	International Accounting Standard Committee
IASB	International Accounting Standards Board
MOU	Memorandum of Understanding
PCAOB	Public Companies Accounting Oversight Board
SAC	Standards Advisory Council
SIC	Standards Interpretation Committee
SEC	Securities and Exchange Commission

APPENDIX B: IFRS TIMELINE

YEAR	ACTION
2001	The IASB is established.
2002	The European Union (EU) announces member states must use IFRS beginning in 2005.
	The IASAB and FASB formally agree to undertake efforts to converge U.S. GAAP and IFRS (The "Norwalk Agreement").
2005	The SEC releases a roadmap for allowing IFRS filings without GAAP reconciliation for foreign firms by 2009, or earlier.
2006	The IASB and FASB agree to work major projects jointly, reaffirming the "Norwalk Agreement."
2007	The SEC announces foreign filers in the United States can file IFRS statements without reconciliation to U.S. GAAP.
2008	The SEC releases updated Roadmap for moving U.S. Companies to IFRS.
	The AICPA's governing council amends its Code of Professional Conduct to recognize the IASB as issuing high quality standards on a par with the FASB.
2009	The SEC will seek large company volunteers to convert to IFRS on a trial basis. The cost is estimated at $32 million per company.
2010–2011	The first U.S. issuers potentially have the ability to use IFRS for SEC reporting purposes.
2011	Canadian, Indian, and Japanese companies are slated to begin using IFRS.
2012	The SEC decides whether to follow for mandating use of IFRS for U.S. public companies.
2013–2017	Phased-in requirement to use IFRS by U.S. public companies if the SEC decides to go forward.

APPENDIX C: CURRENT IFRS AND IAS
As of January 1, 2009

Introduction
Preface to International Financial Reporting Standards
Framework for the Preparation and Presentation of Financial Statements

IFRS 1	First-time Adoption of International Financial Reporting Standards
IFRS 2	Share-based Payment
IFRS 3	Business Combinations
IFRS 4	Insurance Contracts
IFRS 5	Non-current Assets Held for Sale and Discontinued Operations
IFRS 6	Exploration for and Evaluation of Mineral Resources
IFRS 7	Financial Instruments: Disclosures
IFRS 8	Operating Segments
IAS 1	Presentation of Financial Statements
IAS 2	Inventories
IAS 7	Cash Flow Statements
IAS 8	Accounting Policies, Changes in Accounting Estimates and Errors
IAS 10	Events after the Balance Sheet Date
IAS 11	Construction Contracts
IAS 12	Income Taxes
IAS 16	Property, Plant and Equipment
IAS 17	Leases
IAS 18	Revenue
IAS 19	Employee Benefits
IAS 20	Accounting for Government Grants and Disclosure of Government Assistance
IAS 21	The Effects of Changes in Foreign Exchange Rates
IAS 23	Borrowing Costs
IAS 24	Related Party Disclosures
IAS 26	Accounting and Reporting by Retirement Benefit Plans
IAS 27	Consolidated and Separate Financial Statements
IAS 28	Investments in Associates
IAS 29	Financial Reporting in Hyperinflationary Economies
IAS 31	Interests in Joint Ventures
IAS 32	Financial Instruments: Presentation
IAS 33	Earnings per Share
IAS 34	Interim Financial Reporting
IAS 36	Impairment of Assets
IAS 37	Provisions, Contingent Liabilities and Contingent Assets
IAS 38	Intangible Assets
IAS 39	Financial Instruments: Recognition and Measurement
IAS 40	Investment Property
IAS 41	Agriculture

There are also 16 (2 superceded) International Financial Reporting Interpretations (IFRIC) and 11 active pronouncements of the Standards Interpretation Committee (SIC).

APPENDIX D: SELECTED WEBSITES
WITH IFRS RESOURCES

ORGANIZATIONS

IASB http://www.iasb.org (The IASB website includes information on the organization, background on IFRS and summaries of the current standards. Full text of the standards and interpretations are available by subscription.)

FASB http://asc.fasb.org (Click on international)

IAAER http://www.iaaer.org (Full members, $25 annually and student members, $20 annually have free access to the full text of the standards and interpretations.)

AICPA http://www.ifrs.com (The AICPA site with online videos and a list of resources and CPE offerings)

SEC http://www.sec.gov (Click on Global Accounting standards in left column)

ACCOUNTING FIRMS

BDO Seidman http://www.bdo.com (Click on IFRS Resource Center)

Deloitte http://www.deloitte.com (Click on issues and International Financial Reporting Standards (IFRS) including webcast); **http://www.iasplus.com** (Another Deloitte site with extensive resources)

Ernst & Young http://www.eyonline.ey.com (Click on perspectives/overview/IFRS)

Grant Thornton http://www.gtexperience.com (Login: initial of first name+last name: jdoe click on faculty curriculum resources)

KPMG http://www.kpmgifrg.com and http://www.kpmgifrsinstitute.com (KPMG's online IFRS library and resources)

PriceWaterhouseCoopers http://www.pwc.com (Search on IFRS, go to IFRS home page)